D 33- SMOKE BOX

34- „   STACK

35- STEAM DOME

R 36- „   PIPE

K. 37- STOKER FEED

38- SUPERHEATER

39- SIDE RODS—FT. & BK.

40- „   „   —INT.

41- TENDER TRUCK-LEADING

42- „   COAL SPACE

43- „   MAIN FRAME

44- „   WATER TANK

45- TIRE—DRIVING

46- THROTLE OPERATING ROD

47- TRAILING TRUCK BRAKE CYL.

48- „   „   BOX

49- TURRET VALVE CASING

50- VALVE MOTION COMBINATION LEVER

51- „   „   CRANK

52- „   „   ECCENTRIC ROD

53- „   „   LINK

54- „   „   RADIUS ROD

55- „   ROD

56- WHISTLE

OCOMOTIVE

Nicknamed "BIG BOY"

Boiler pressure—300 lbs. per sq. inch

Maximum tractive power—135,375 lbs.

Tender Type—14 Wheeled. Water capacity—25,000 gallons

Fuel—28 tons Soft Coal

FOREWORD

Having, since the age of four, always been interested in railroads, their motive power, signals, train dispatching, yard facilities, maintenance of way and everything else that is included in their magnificent all-round operation, it has always been in the back of my mind to try to write a book that would not only thrill the youngsters but would be of interest to all ages of both sexes. I wanted it to be the type of book that I would have liked to read many times during my life and also one that would answer many of the questions that have been put to me.

With the able assistance of Glen Thomas, one of this country's leading illustrators who specializes in railroad and transportation work, I am hopeful that we have accomplished in a small way a book that will prove helpful to the American public.

I have the rare good fortune to number friends among the officials of almost all of the Class 1 American railroads and therefore, have been given permission to ride locomotives and freight trains, besides having the opportunity of spending much time in railroad offices and on their property looking over their operations at first hand.

On page 23 and 24, the reader will find abstracts taken from a leading railroad's book of rules — a volume that none of the public ever sees — and these pages should prove informative and help to solve some of the perplexed looks I have seen on many travelers riding the American railroads, both in war and peace time. These two pages I also trust will be enjoyed by the members of our armed forces as they move from one railroad to another in the various states of the Union.

It seems appropriate to me and I am particularly pleased that this book should make its appearance when the American railroads are performing the greatest job in the history of transportation and have so ably proved themselves the first line of the nation's defenses. The great improvements that they added to their properties in peacetime depression years have certainly paid dividends to the people of the United States in contributing to the war effort of this world conflagration.

I am particularly indebted to the American Locomotive Company, The Baldwin Locomotive Works, the Electro-Motive Corporation, the Lima Locomotive Works, the Union Switch and Signal Company, and the Railway Age magazine for their kind help and cooperation in aiding me to complete the book.

I appreciate greatly the many courtesies tendered me by my friends of the various railroads that are in the book and I am only sorry that it is not possible to cover all the railroads, their motive power and trains which I would like to have represented here.

In conclusion, I must also thank Mr. Glen Thomas for his grand job and cooperation in the way he handled the art work in the book. His was a much harder job than mine.

S. KIP FARRINGTON, Jr.

East Hampton, New York
July 5, 1944

GIANTS OF THE RAILS

BY S. KIP FARRINGTON, JR.

ILLUSTRATIONS *by*

Glen Thomas

GARDEN CITY PUBLISHING COMPANY, INC., GARDEN CITY, N.Y.

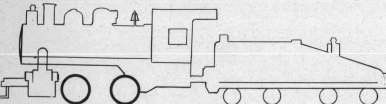

0-4-0 TYPE 4-WHEEL SWITCHER — Used for light switching on industrial tracks where clearances are limited. Engine built for Penn. R.R.

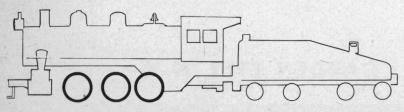

0-6-0 TYPE 6-WHEEL SWITCHER — Used in passenger as well as freight service. This one also built for Penn. R.R.

TWENTIETH CENTURY LIMITED

New York Central No. 25, the westbound Twentieth Century Limited, running over the Hudson Division on a fine spring evening. The Century is probably the most famous train in the world and many people believe it to be the premiere train of the east. It is an all room train and its wartime makeup consists of seventeen cars, thirteen of them carrying revenue passengers and every berth is always filled. Two dining cars go through the entire distance and their crews sleep in the dormitory at the head end of the lounge car at the front of the train. A working post office car is ahead of that next to the engine. An observation lounge car with two master bedrooms is at the rear end. The streamlined engine No. 5454, 4-6-4 Type Class J-3A above is the latest edition of the famous Hudson Type that was designed and first used by the New York Central in 1926. This engine will run right through from Harmon, New York, where the electric engine from Grand Central Station is cut off, to Toledo, Ohio, a distance of 695 miles but on occasions the engines go through to Chicago. Coal is taken at Wayneport, New York, 323 miles from Harmon, and water is scooped from track pans at 19 places without stopping between Harmon and Chicago, both east and westbound.

THE YANKEE

PENNSYLVANIA R. R.

The Yankee is one of the finest and fastest of the Pennsylvania Railroad's great fleet of preference freight trains which are all named and carry a symbol. The Yankee carries a great
deal of freight from New England for points west which is delivered by the New Haven Railroad via car ferry at Greenville, New Jersey, from the New Haven Terminal at Bay Ridge, New
York. The Yankee then runs as P-5 to the great classification yard at Enola, Pennsylvania, just
outside of Harrisburg, where cars from Philadelphia and Baltimore are added, and it continues
right through to Chicago as Train NL-1 with third morning delivery at that point from the Atlantic
seaboard and New England. The engine No. 6846 is a Mountain or 4-8-2 Type built in 1930
and the water capacity of its tender is 22,000 gallons. It was one of the first large tanks put
into service on an American railroad. The author has ridden two of these engines double-heading
this train from Greenville to Enola, 188 miles, with 121 cars weighing 6180 tons in the
remarkable time of five hours and fifteen minutes. Only one stop was made the entire distance
and that for the two locomotives to take coal. Water is also scooped up while running over track
tanks as they are called on the Pennsylvania. This is moving fast freight with a vengeance.

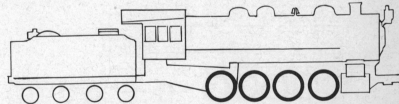

0-8-0 TYPE 8-WHEEL SWITCHER for freight switching in classification yards. This
one belongs to Lackawanna R.R.

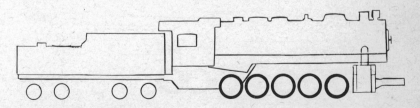

0-10-0 TYPE—10-WHEEL SWITCHER for the very heaviest switching service. This engine
built for C. & O. Ry.

0-10-2 TYPE — built for and used only by the Union R.R. in heavy transfer and switching service.

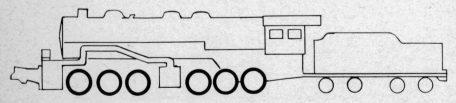

0-6-6-0 TYPE — used for heavy service in hump and flat yards. Belongs to N.Y.C. None built in recent years.

GOLDBALL AND ROCKY MOUNTAIN ROCKET CHICAGO, ROCK ISLAND AND PACIFIC RY.

The Rock Island Rocky Mountain Rocket train No. 7 westbound from Chicago to Denver an Colorado Springs has overtaken and is about to pass No. 91, crack Rock Island Time Freigh east of Joliet, Illinois. No. 7 is hauled by a two unit 4000 H.P. Diesel electric passenger loco motive which will run right through from Chicago to Denver, a distance of 1083 miles. This train one of the great fleet of streamlined Rockets that are in service all over the Rock Island Lin and are some of the most modern high speed trains operating in the United States.

The California Goldball is hauled by engine No. 2590 2-8-2 Type Class K-64 which w handle the train from Burr Oak Yards, Chicago, to Silvis, Illinois, a distance of 174 miles. He the greater part of all westbound classification is carried on. Colorado-California No. 91 make connection with the Rio Grande at Denver where it becomes the Ute into Salt Lake City, thenc over the Western Pacific to Pacific Coast terminals in the Bay District of San Francisco.

The Rock Island has recently put in service some 5400 H.P. Freight Diesels and have ju received some new 4-8-4 Type oil burning dual service engines to supplement their large fle of modernized 4-8-4s. They also own some heavy 2-10-2 Type engines.

EASTBOUND FAST FREIGHT NO. 424   GREAT NORTHERN RY.

The Great Northern Ry. is using some 2 Unit 2700 H.P. Diesel electric freight locomotives in road service. Here is one descending grade just west of Glacier Park on an early March morning with the Eastbound Fast Freight No. 424. The train has just crossed the Continental Divide at Summit coming over the Rocky Mountains through the famous Marias Pass. The train consists of 72 cars, totaling 3250 tons, and the helping engine No. 2051 2-8-8-2 Type Class R-2 was cut off at Summit after assisting the Diesel from Whitefish. This train is enroute to Minneapolis and St. Paul, Minnesota. At 6:20 P.M. the evening of this same day the famous Empire Builder, leading passenger train of the Great Northern between Seattle, Spokane, the twin cities and Chicago, will also be descending this grade and will be followed at midnight by No. 28, the Eastbound Fast Mail. The freight Diesels have been used a great deal in helping service on both the east and west slope of the Continental Divide on the Great Northern and have given a very satisfactory account of themselves for their adaptability for this work just as they have in road service. This is the Second Subdivision of the Kalispell Division, extending from Whitefish to Blackfoot, Montana.

0-8-8-0 TYPE — built for pushing heavy coal and ore trains over humps. None recently built. Owned by Penn. R.R.

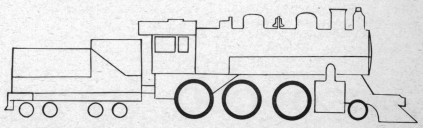

2-6-0 MOGUL TYPE — once America's largest freight engine. None built for many years. This one owned by S. P. System.

2-8-0 CONSOLIDATION TYPE — followed Mogul as standard American freight engine. None built in recent years. Reading Ry. owns this one.

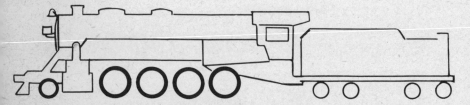

2-10-0 DECAPOD TYPE — used in heavy slow freight and drag service, usually hauling coal and ore. Engine built for Western Maryland Ry.

CHESAPEAKE & OHIO COAL TRAIN

Many times every twenty-four hours a solid coal train, each one totaling 160 loaded cars averaging 13,500 tons, leaves the Chesapeake & Ohio's stupendous classification yards at Russell, Kentucky for Columbus and Toledo, Ohio. At the latter point, coal is loaded into lake vessels from the magnificent Presque Isle coal loading terminal for delivery by water to northern ports. The Russell, Kentucky Yard is the largest coal classification yard in the United States and boasts two gravity hump yards, car retarders, track scales and extensive engine terminals and shops for repairing coal cars. This engine No. 3032 2-10-4 Type is one of 40 built by the Lima Locomotive Works in 1930 that are used in a pool assigned only to this service. They handle the train right through from Russell to Toledo, a distance of 243 miles. They are given assistance when hauling this heavy tonnage for 21 miles after leaving Russell to N. J. Cabin, Ky. where the Ohio River is crossed on a magnificent bridge to South Portsmouth, Ohio by a 2-8-8-2 Type Class H-7A locomotive pusher at the rear end. This is one of the greatest operations performed by any railroad or locomotive in the United States.

THE UTE

DENVER & RIO GRANDE WESTERN R. R.

The Rio Grande's Ute No. 61 climbing the 2% grade west of Fireclay, Colorado enroute to the Moffatt Tunnel. The Rio Grande uses the tracks of the Denver & Salt Lake from Denver to Bond, Colo., as this short cut saves 175 miles, heavy grades and much curvature over the route through the Royal Gorge and Tennessee Pass. The Moffat Tunnel Line is also used by the Expedition Flyer No. 5 and No. 6, the pride of the Rio Grande passenger service. The engine No. 3602 2-8-8-2 Type Class L-131 will run through to Grand Junction, 274 miles, and the pusher, out of sight at the rear end, will be cut off at the east portal of the Moffat Tunnel 50 miles from Denver.

The Ute carries fast freight of all kinds received from the Chicago, Burlington and Quincy and Rock Island at Denver and the train usually covers the 570 miles from Denver to Salt Lake City in from twenty to twenty-four hours. This is excellent time for mountain railroading as No. 61 will have to climb the Wahsatch Mountains from Helper to Soldier, Summit, Utah, where for 13 miles the ruling grade is 2.40%.

The Moffat Tunnel itself ranks sixth in length of the great tunnels of the world and second in the U.S., being exceeded only by the Cascade Tunnel on the Great Northern in Washington; it is 6.09 miles long and pierces the Continental Divide at an elevation of 9200 ft. The eastern portal of the Tunnel is approached by the long 2% grade and for a distance of 11 miles there are 28 tunnels and new and startling panoramas constantly unfold.

2-6-2 PRAIRIE TYPE — popular with many western roads after turn of the century. None built for many years. Engine above owned by C. B. & Q. R.R.

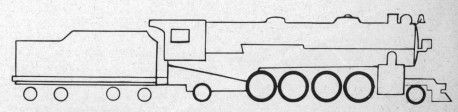

2-8-2 MIKADO TYPE — now called MacArthur on some roads since Dec. 7, 1941. This engine built for Southern Ry.

2-10-2 SANTA FE TYPE — first used on that system — hence its name. Popular type for freight service where grades are heavy. This engine built for Missouri Pacific R.R.

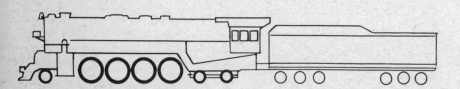

2-8-4 BERKSHIRE TYPE — modern high speed freight engine becoming more popular every year. This one built for R. F. & P. R.R.

FAST MAIL AND EXPRESS

Probably the most famous and fastest of the great trains which literally and figuratively carry the mail are Santa Fe No. 7 and 8. It is the only mail train running through west of the Missouri River to California under one management and has been in operation since 1897. Carrying Uncle Sam's mail and express is one of the most important jobs that the railroads do and everything possible is done to expedite this service. No. 7 and 8 are operated in two sections and the first one is limited to twelve cars in both directions and the running time is 49 hours and 25 minutes westbound and 53 hours and 20 minutes eastbound, the slight difference being due to the change in time.

The artist has portrayed the train here just west of Winslow, Arizona on the Third District of the Albuquerque Division with a beautiful Arizona sunset in the western sky.

The engine No. 3784 4-8-4 Type of the great Santa Fe 3776 Class, built by the Baldwin Locomotive Works, is one of two equipped with Timken roller bearing rods, a fine new feature that should mean a great deal to prolonging the life of the steam locomotive. The 3784 is running through from Los Angeles, California to La Junta, Colorado, a distance of 1234 miles with this train.

NEW ENGLAND STATES OIL TRAIN.　　　　　BOSTON AND ALBANY R. R.

Among the most important of the railroads many magnificent contributions to the war effort, none have been more vital than their handling of the oil movement to the eastern seaboard. Prior to the war, ocean tanker delivery of oil to the Atlantic coastal states accounted for over 95% of the total reaching this territory. At this time deliveries by sea have shrunk to less than 15% with over 85% depending on movement by the railroads. No railroad has a better record than the New York Central in handling oil and the Boston & Albany, which is a part of that system, has done its share for the New England states.

The picture shows a solid oil train, double headed with two of the original 2-8-4 Berkshire Type Boston & Albany Class A-1 working hard at Charlton, Massachusetts. This engine was first put in service on the B & A which runs through the Berkshire Hills from whence the locomotive received its name. These engines have done excellent work on various other roads including the Boston & Maine, Erie, Santa Fe, Illinois Central, Louisville & Nashville, Chicago & North Western, Missouri Pacific, Pere Marquette, Nickel Plate, Chesapeake & Ohio, Wheeling and Lake Erie, Detroit, Toledo and Ironton and Richmond, Fredericksburg & Potomac.

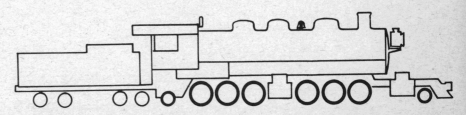

2-10-4 TEXAS TYPE — another modern high speed heavy tonnage freight engine. Belongs to Texas & Pacific Ry.

2-6-6-2 TYPE — used in heavy mountain freight service — none built in recent years. Belongs to Great Northern Ry.

2-8-8-0 TYPE — generally used for hauling heavy coal and ore trains where grades are heavy. This one built for B. & O. R.R.

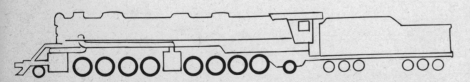

2-8-8-2 TYPE — very popular for hauling the heaviest tonnage trains in mountain territory. This engine belongs to Rio Grande R.R.

PACIFIC LIMITED NO. 21   SOUTHERN PACIFIC LINES

Southern Pacific engine No. 4124 Class AC-5 4-8-8-2 Type. This locomotive is the famous cab ahead articulated consolidation type which is used only on the Southern Pacific who have over 200 in service. The design and performance of this locomotive has been one of the most outstanding in the history of the United States and they are used with excellent results in passenger as well as freight service in the many mountain districts in which the Southern Pacific operates. Due to the fact that they are oil burners, it is practical to run them cab first, thus enabling the cab to remain clear of smoke and fumes from the exhaust when running through the many tunnels and snowsheds that are encountered in mountain territory and also increasing the visibility thus aiding greatly to the comfort and efficiency of the engine crew.

The westbound Pacific Limited is pictured coming out of a snowshed skirting historic Donner Lake while climbing the east slope of the Sierra Nevadas on the westward track, just east of Summit, Calif. The grade here is 2½%. These engines will haul 1850 tons unassisted westbound on this section of the Sacramento Division. The heaviest snowfall and some of the coldest weather in this country are found here on the "hill" as the S.P. men affectionately call it and they may well be pardoned for their pride in this operation as it is one of the world's finest.

SUPER CHIEF NO. 18   **ATCHISON, TOPEKA & SANTA FE RY.**

Many railroads, particularly in mountain territory, use the left hand operation usually as a means of reducing steep grades; while others, like the picture on the opposite page, while using double track for both eastward and westward movement do not have them paralleling one another. Above you see the Santa Fe Super Chief, only deluxe all Pullman twice weekly steamliner from Chicago to Los Angeles. It is shown here being hauled by two 2000 H.P. Electro-Motive Diesel passenger locomotives at Gonzales, New Mexico, on the First District of the Santa Fe's Albuquerque Division. This is the top of the Continental Divide with an elevation of 7248 Ft. It marks the watershed, as from here east and west the waters flow to the Gulf of Mexico and Atlantic on one hand and to the Gulf of California and the Pacific on the other.

The Super Chief leaves Chicago Tuesdays and Saturdays and makes the run to Los Angeles in 41¾ hours; its schedule having been lengthened two hours on account of the war. Eastbound it leaves Los Angeles Tuesdays and Fridays. Its wartime makeup consists of 14 cars, including a beautiful dormitory baggage lounge car on the head end, a dormitory lounge car next to the dining car in the middle of the train besides the observation lounge on the rear end.

Note the Hopi Indian village on the south side of the tracks.

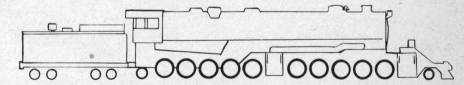

2-10-10-2 TYPE — built for and used only on the Virginian Ry. for hauling the heaviest coal trains.

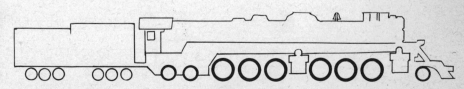

2-6-6-4 TYPE — in service on three American roads hauling fast manifest freight trains. This one built for Seaboard R.R.

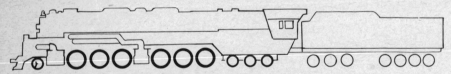

2-6-6-6 ALLEGHENY TYPE — built for and used only on the Chesapeake & Ohio Ry. where it has proved a great success.

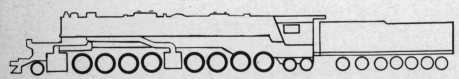

2-8-8-4 YELLOWSTONE TYPE — so named because it was first used on Northern Pacific. This one belongs to Duluth, Missabe & Iron Range Ry.

EASTBOUND STOCK TRAIN
ATCHISON, TOPEKA & SANTA FE RY.

The transportation of livestock to the various markets is one of the most exacting jobs that the American railroads undertake. The best of care and attention must be given our four-legged friends, most of whom are getting their first and last ride as passengers on a railroad car. If the railroads were to fall down in their care of this movement, Mr. John Q. Public could easily miss his favorite steak or roast on the days he chooses to order it. The problem of the railroad is to make certain that the stock arrives on time. Animals arriving on the market after the buyers have finished for the day must be held over until the following market day. This involves feeding costs and often a decline in the quality of the animals offered for sale. Animals in transit must be unloaded, fed and watered after they have been enroute thirty-six hours. The Santa Fe owns 7900 stock cars, 62 of which are here rolling smoothly behind engine 5004 2-10-4 Texas Type west of Vaughn on the Pecos Division in the middle of a wonderful New Mexico night. This engine gets its name because it was first used on the Texas & Pacific, is one of the Santa Fe 5001 Class, has the longest one-piece engine bed of any locomotive in the U. S. and is also the only 10 coupled locomotive having driving wheels over 70 inches.

TRAIL BLAZER NO. 77

PENNSYLVANIA R. R.

The Pennsylvania Railroad's New York Division between New York and Philadelphia, is the world's busiest piece of railroad. The road's electrified territory also extends through to Washington, D. C., and Harrisburg, Pa. with many branches and low grade freight lines also equipped for this type of operation.

Above we see one of the famous GG-1's westbound with the Trail Blazer No. 77 deluxe all-coach train between New York and Chicago running 80 miles an hour west of Princeton Junction, N. J. The track here is laid with 152 pound rail, heaviest used in the United States. This type of overnight low cost deluxe coach travel, first introduced on the Union Pacific with its famous fleet of Challengers, has proved just as popular in wartime as it did in peacetime and the Santa Fe El Capitan and Scout; Rock Island-Southern Pacific Californian; New York Central Pacemaker; Atlantic Coast Line Champion; Pennsylvania Jeffersonian; Baltimore & Ohio Columbian; the Seaboard Silver Meteor; as well as other deluxe coach trains carrying light weight Pullman equipment are all filled to capacity. The GG-1 is the engine which is handling 15 to 17 cars every hour from New York to Washington and also runs the hourly trains between New York and Philadelphia. They are geared for a maximum speed of 100 miles per hour.

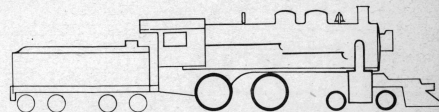

4-4-0 AMERICAN TYPE — the first successful American passenger engine. None built for many years. This one belongs to Reading Ry.

4-6-0—10-WHEEL TYPE — very popular in early 1900's — still used by many roads in suburban and local service. This one built for Atlantic Coast Line R.R.

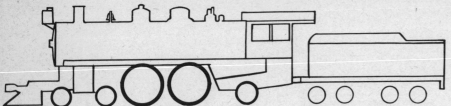

4-4-2 ATLANTIC TYPE — first used on Atlantic Coast Line — hence its name. Fastest engine of its day. Above engine built for Frisco Lines.

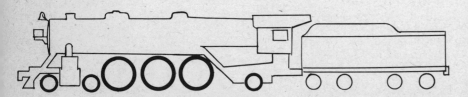

4-6-2 PACIFIC TYPE — none recently built but still more in passenger service than any other type. Built for Erie R.R.

HAVANA SPECIAL   RICHMOND, FREDERICKSBURG AND POTOMAC R.R.

The Richmond, Fredericksburg & Potomac is the biggest little road in the country — only 113 miles in length — it is the connecting link between Washington and Richmond that all Atlantic Coast Line and Seaboard Railroad connections, both freight and passenger, to and from the Pennsylvania and Baltimore & Ohio from north of Washington run over. It is owned by the Pennsylvania, Baltimore & Ohio, Atlantic Coast Line, Chesapeake & Ohio, Southern, Seaboard, also a few minority stockholders and the state of Virginia, is magnificently maintained and operated. Its automatic signals and train control are some of the best in the United States and its track is laid with 131 pound rail. The road's Potomac Yard is one of the finest and most up-to-date classification yards in the East. It has marvelous motive power which is kept in excellent shape. Its five 4-8-4 Type used in freight service are named after the famous southern generals, Lee, Jackson, Stuart, A. P. Hill and J. E. Johnston and the dozen used in passenger service are named after former celebrated governors of the state of Virginia. Ten more of these engines are now on order.

Above we see engine No. 604, the Governor Benjamin Harrison, crossing the bridge over Occoquan Creek, Virginia, with the Washington section of the Atlantic Coast Line's Havana Special No. 376 enroute from Miami and other west and east coast Florida points to the Nation's Capital.

WAR FREIGHT FOR THE WEST COAST   UNION PACIFIC R. R.

Nothing can ever be written that could come anywhere near giving credit to the railroads of the United States for the way they have handled the transportation of war freight in World War II. Not a ship has been launched, not a single item of Lend Lease food or equipment sent overseas without first having begun their journey as raw material or finished product some-where, sometime on a steel rail and the same also can be said for every soldier or sailor who went overseas. The majority of freight trains are run as extras and therefore the locomotives carry white flags by day and white classification lights at night and here you can see that the X before the engine number on the train indicator denotes the train is not scheduled in the operating time table.

Here is the latest Union Pacific 4-6-6-4 Challenger Type named for their low-cost coach train because it was the first of a great number of a very popular type to be used on many American railroads. All of them have turned in a very handsome job in both freight and pas-senger service. Above we see Extra No. 3950 in beautiful Echo Canyon, Utah, on the Eighth Subdivision of the Wyoming Division between Evanston and Ogden. The engine has come through from Green River.

4-8-2 MOUNTAIN TYPE — a most successful type for both fast freight and heavy passenger service. This engine built for Boston & Maine R.R.

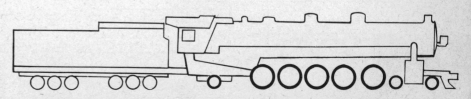

4-10-2 SOUTHERN PACIFIC TYPE — first built for S.P. and the only other road to follow them was U.P. Used in heavy freight service. Owned by S.P. System.

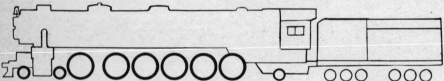

4-12-2 UNION PACIFIC TYPE — built for and used only by Union Pacific in fast freight service.

4-6-4 HUDSON TYPE — today's most popular high speed passenger engine where grades are moderate. This engine built for New Haven R.R.

HIAWATHA   **CHICAGO, MILWAUKEE, ST. PAUL AND PACIFIC R. R.**

The first Hiawatha was a great Mohawk chieftain of the sixteenth century who affected the confederation known as the Five Nations or League of the Iroquois. Miraculous powers and deeds were ascribed to him in legend. The Hiawathas of today leave Chicago and the Twin Cities every morning and afternoon on the Milwaukee Railroad. The afternoon Hiawathas, trains No. 100 and 101, make the run of 420.8 miles in seven hours and cover the 85 miles between Chicago and Milwaukee in seventy-five minutes.

Above we see this beautiful train being hauled by engine No. 100 4-6-4 Hudson Type Class F-7. This locomotive, along with the C. & N.W. Class E-4 and the Santa Fe 3460 Class, like the one pictured on the cover of this book with the Chief, all three being of this Type are the only American locomotives with 84 inch driving wheels. These three classes of locomotives are the fastest in service at this time. They all have 300 pound boiler pressure and the Santa Fe 3460 Class burn oil. The author has ridden 117 miles an hour on one of the last named, the fastest he has ever ridden on any locomotive at any time. The Milwaukee F-7's are also used on the crack Olympian as far west as Harlowton, Montana, the Pioneer Limited and the Fast Mail which handles all the mail and express from the western connections out of St. Paul and Minneapolis between Chicago and those cities.

CALIFORNIA TEXAS FAST FREIGHT

ATCHISON, TOPEKA & SANTA FE RY.

The First District of the Santa Fe's Arizona Division from Needles, California to Seligman, Arizona is 149.7 miles. The elevation at Needles is just 476 feet above sea level. Seligman stands at 5234 feet, almost one mile high. The grade is 1.5% for 126 miles from Needles to Yampai with the exception of 12 miles from Louise to Walapai where it varies from level to a trifle more than 0.5%. The last 23 miles from Yampaï to Seligman varies from 1 to 1.5%. This is the longest, hardest sustained grade of any railroad in the United States. This is also the longest steam helper district in the country.

The 5400 H.P. 4 Unit Santa Fe freight Diesels, like the one pictured above with the eastbound CTX (California Texas Fast Freight), climbing the grade east of Hackberry, handle 3500 tons unassisted over this District up this long punishing pull in from six to seven hours with two stops for inspection of the train. The Santa Fe has 48 of these Freight Diesels in service as well as 15 passenger and 117 Diesel switch engines. The freight Diesels run through from Barstow, California to Winslow, Arizona, a total of 460 tough miles. These freight Diesels are well suited for operation on the Santa Fe due to the elimination of long hauls by tank cars of water in the desert districts of Arizona for steam motive power.

4-8-4 NORTHERN TYPE — most popular dual service locomotive ever built. First used by Northern Pacific for whom this engine operates.

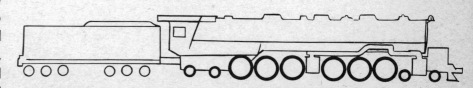

4-6-6-4 CHALLENGER TYPE — used in both high speed freight and passenger service where grades are heavy. This one built for Western Pacific.

4-8-8-2 ARTICULATED CONSOLIDATION TYPE — amazingly successful cab ahead oil burning locomotive built and used only by S.P. System.

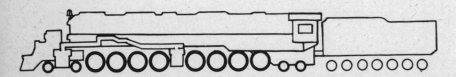

4-8-8-4 TYPE — built and used only by the Union Pacific. This locomotive — world's heaviest — proved highly successful.

THE DAYLIGHT

The Southern Pacific's beautiful Daylight, train No. 98, one of America's finest streamliners, running between San Francisco and Los Angeles, wartime makeup consists of 20 cars. Following the romantic El Camino Real — the King's Highway that linked the chain of early California Missions — this train traverses the rich Santa Clara Valley, famous for its prunes and apricots; the Salinas Valley, known as the "Salad Bowl of America," where is grown much of our lettuce; passes through the Santa Lucia Mountains over Santa Margarita to San Luis Obispo, which means "St. Louis the Bishop." South from San Luis Obispo the Daylight skirts the Pacific Ocean for over 100 miles and is shown here near Concepcion on the Coast Division with engine No. 4417 4-8-4 Type Class GS-3. At Ventura, south of Santa Barbara, oil wells are noted in the ocean and then upon leaving the sea the Daylight passes enormous orange groves. Arriving at Los Angeles the traveler's eye is taken by the magnificent Union Station — high ceilinged and spacious, its decoration being entirely that of early California, it is probably the most beautiful passenger station in America. The companion train, the San Joaquin Daylight, also operates every day via Bakersfield and the famous Tahachapi Loop.

EASTBOUND CALIFORNIA FRUIT

UNION PACIFIC R. R.

The Union Pacific 4000 Class 4-8-8-4 Type, the world's heaviest locomotives, are in service between Ogden, Utah, and Green River, Wyoming, a distance of 175.6 miles. The heaviest grade eastbound is 1.14% between Uintah and Gateway, Echo and Baskin, Emory and Wahsatch as they pull up over the beautiful range of the last named place. Westbound the ruling grade is .82% between Green River and Peru, and Leroy to Aspen, the location of the Union Pacific's longest tunnel. These great locomotives, built by the American Locomotive Company, can handle unassisted, 3800 tons eastbound and 4900 tons westbound. The maximum cylinder horsepower is 7000 and is reached at approximately 45 miles per hour and carries on to 60 miles per hour.

Engine 4006 is shown here with an eastbound perishable fruit train from California west of Wahsatch. The handling of citrus fruits is just one more grand service the American railroads render the citizens of the United States, as the utmost care must be taken in safeguarding them against weather conditions and extreme changes in temperature. This engine will take water at Echo, Evanston and Carter and coal at Evanston.

2-C + C-2 TYPE — used on all passenger trains and some freight in Pennsylvania's electrified territory.

2-C-1 + 1-C-2 TYPE — built for and used for hauling all passenger trains by Milwaukee R.R. between Harlowton, Mont., and Avery, Idaho.

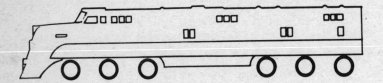

2000 H.P. DIESEL ELECTRIC PASSENGER LOCOMOTIVE A-UNIT — used alone for hauling light trains. This Diesel belongs to Florida East Coast Ry.

4000 H.P. DIESEL ELECTRIC PASSENGER LOCOMOTIVE A AND B UNITS — most popular passenger combination. This Diesel built for Illinois Central System.

THE CITY OF SAN FRANCISCO

UNION PACIFIC R. R.

The City of San Francisco, deluxe coach and Pullman streamliner, operates every third day in both directions between Chicago and San Francisco over the Chicago and North Western, Union Pacific and Southern Pacific Railroads. This striking all yellow train from the head end of its 3 Unit 6000 H.P. Diesel to the marker lights at the rear end of the last car is painted complete with that vivid color. Its wartime makeup is seventeen cars. The artist has given us a fine reproduction of No. 101, the westbound City of San Francisco running through a heavy electrical storm on an early summer morning just east of North Platte, Nebraska, on the Second Subdivision of the Nebraska Division.

The railroads are used to hauling trains through all kinds of weather conditions from heavy snowstorms and sub-zero weather in the winter to cloudbursts and tornadoes in the summer months. A very true inscription from Herodotus completely describes the service they render — "Neither snow, nor rain, nor heat, nor gloom of night stays these couriers from the swift completion of their appointed rounds."

EASTBOUND MANIFEST NO. 94

Chesapeake and Ohio No. 94 is another of the crack fast freight trains that are operating on so many railroads in the United States. Different lines give them different names — fast freight, symbol freight, preference freight, time freight, manifest freight, through freight and merchandisers, but they all mean the same. Few of us have, perhaps, paused to realize of the many things that reach us in a freight car, the materials of which houses and apartments are made, our furniture, the car we drive, the gasoline that propels it, the tools of trade and profession, luxury and necessity — almost every commodity under the sun.

The Chicago and Toledo sections of No. 94 run as two sections to Clifton Forge, Virginia where the train is re-classified for Washington through Potomac Yard and points north and for Newport News and Norfolk through Richmond, Virginia. The engine is the 2-6-6-6 or Allegheny Type, so-called because they are only used on the C. & O. They are classified H-8 by this road. With the exception of one experimental engine, built for the Pennsylvania which was on exhibit at the New York World's Fair, they are the only locomotives in service today that are equipped with a 6-wheel trailing truck.

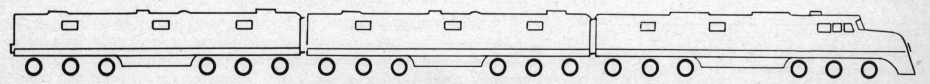

6000 H.P. DIESEL ELECTRIC PASSENGER LOCOMOTIVE A, B AND C UNITS — generally used for hauling trains with 15 or more cars. This one is owned by Chicago and North Western System.

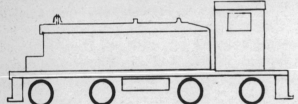

600 H.P. DIESEL ELECTRIC SWITCHING LOCOMOTIVE — used in both freight and passenger service. This Diesel owned by Lehigh Valley R.R.

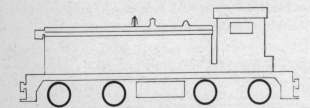

1000 H.P. DIESEL ELECTRIC SWITCHING LOCOMOTIVE — used in heavy switching and transfer service. This Diesel belongs to the Louisville & Nashville R.R.

N & W TIME FREIGHT NO. 99   NORFOLK AND WESTERN RY.

Here we see westbound Time Freight, No. 99 one of the three crack freight trains of the Norfolk & Western, passing the plant of the Wheeling Steel Company at South Portsmouth, Ohio, on the Scioto Division. This locomotive No. 1200 is of the 2-6-6-4 Type Norfolk & Western Class A and was built in the magnificent Roanoke shops of that road at Roanoke, Virginia. These engines are giving a great account of themselves in handling all the Time Freight, many of the heavy coal trains and in heavy passenger and troop train service.

The author has ridden this train from Roanoke, Virginia, to Portsmouth, Ohio, with only one stop other than at regular operating points and that only to let a passenger train run around us, a distance of 312 miles. One of these Class A engines handled the train of 8500 tons from Williamson to Portsmouth, where it is split for Columbus and Cincinnati. The N. & W. headquarters at Roanoke, Virginia, in the beautiful city in the heart of the Blue Ridge Mountains, is one of the many towns and cities in the United States that was started and developed by a railroad and the majority of its inhabitants receive their incomes, in one way or another, from the railroad. The N. & W. boasts some of the finest track in this country.

THE CHIEF

ATCHISON, TOPEKA & SANTA FE RY.

This 4-8-4 type locomotive of the Santa Fe 3776 class and their predecessors, the 3765 class, are duplicates with the exception that the latter were built of heavier alloys and only carry 20,000 gallons of water in their tenders. The 76 class carries 25,000 gallons. These engines as well as the 3751 class, first of this type used on the Santa Fe, run through from Kansas City to Los Angeles, 1788 miles, without change, hauling the California Limited, the Grand Canyon Limited and the Scout. This is the longest run that a steam engine makes in the United States. Oil is used for fuel and the tenders have a capacity of 7041 gallons. Twelve different engine crews handle the train during this run.

Engine 3777 is shown here going into San Bernardino, California, with the eastbound Chief No. 20. The Chief is the only daily all-Pullman deluxe streamliner between Chicago and California and like the Super Chief, is the only other train in this country that carries three lounge cars. During wartime seats are for sale in them. The Chief's regular makeup is 14 cars with an extra car to Phoenix added during the winter months. It also carries two cars of storage mail and a working mail car. It holds the highest place in the hearts of all Santa Fe men of any train that runs over the road and is considered by many people to be America's finest train.

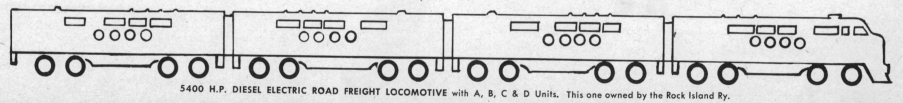

5400 H.P. DIESEL ELECTRIC ROAD FREIGHT LOCOMOTIVE with A, B, C & D Units. This one owned by the Rock Island Ry.

AUTOMATIC BLOCK SEMAPHORE SIGNALS

Three Position Upper Quadrant Type

 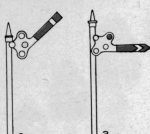 

Home and Distant Lower Quadrant Type

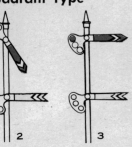

No. 1—**Clear Signal**—Proceed, two or more blocks clear

No. 2—**Approach Signal**—Proceed at reduced speed, prepared to stop at next signal.

No. 3—**Stop Signal**—Stop, then proceed, prepared to stop short of any obstruction.

AUTOMATIC BLOCK POSITION LIGHT SIGNAL

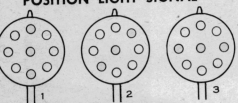

AUTOMATIC BLOCK COLOR LIGHT SIGNAL

AUTOMATIC BLOCK SEARCHLIGHT SIGNAL

No. 1—**Clear Signal**—Proceed two or more blocks clear.

No. 2—**Approach Signal**—Proceed at reduced speed, prepared to stop at next signal.

No. 3—**Stop Signal**—Stop, then proceed, prepared to stop short of any obstruction.

SEARCHLIGHT DWARF SIGNAL

Single lens gives any one of these color indications.
Red—Stop.
Yellow—Proceed restricted speed.
Green—Proceed slow speed within interlocking limits.

TWO POSITION LIGHT DWARF SIGNAL

Two colored lens: Red top, green bottom.
Red top light means stop.
Green bottom light. Proceed slow speed within interlocking limits.

ELECTRO-PNEUMATIC SEMAPHORE DWARF SIGNAL

Semaphore Blade horizontal, red light means stop.
Semaphore Blade 60° downward, yellow light, means proceed at restricted speed. Semaphore Blade inclined 90° downward. Green light. Proceed slow within interlocking limits.

ENGINE WHISTLE SIGNALS

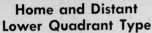

The signals prescribed are illustrated by ''o'' for short sounds, ''—'' for longer sounds; and ''——•—'' for extra long sounds. The sounds of the whistle should be distinct; short sounds should continue for approximately 1½ to 2 seconds, with a stop of one second; long sounds should continue for approximately 2½ to seconds with a stop of one second; extra long sounds should continue for approximately 5 seconds.

SOUND	INDICATION
o	Apply brakes. Stop.
— —	Release brakes. Proceed.
— o o o	Flagman protect rear of train.
— — — —	(Single and double track). Flagman may return from west or south.
— — — — —	(Single and double track). Flagman may return from east or north.
— — — —	When running, train parted; to be repeated until answered by signal prescribed by lamp signal E on lower part of right hand page.
o o	Answer to any signal not otherwise provided for.
o o o	When train is standing, back. Answer to lamp signal D on lower part of right hand page.
o o o o	Call for signals.
— o o	(Single track). To call attention of yard engines, extra trains, or trains of the same or inferior class or inferior right, to signals displayed for following section.
	(Double track). To call attention of yard engines or of trains moving in the same direction to signals displayed for following section.
—— • —— o o	Approaching public crossings at grade, at curves and other obscure places to be prolonged or repeated until passed.
——	Approaching stations, junctions, railroad crossings and tunnels.
o o —	Second engineman on doubleheader assume control of air brakes.
o	Inspect train line for leak, or for brakes sticking.

Succession of short sounds. Alarm for persons or live stock on the track.

COMMUNICATING SIGNALS

(Between train crew and engine crew given only from train by pulling air signal cord in the following manner.)

Sound	Indication
o o	When standing—start
o o	When running—stop at once
o o o	When standing—back the train
o o o	When running—stop at next passenger station
o o o o	When standing—apply or release air brakes
o o o o	When running—reduce speed
o o o o o	When standing—recall flagman
o o o o o	When running—increase speed
o	Conductor call engineman's attention to meeting point
o o o o o o	When running—increase train heat
— o	When running—shut off train heat
	When running—brakes sticking; look back for hand signals

TRAIN SIGNALS

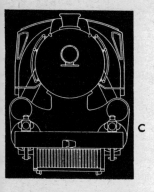

ine running backward by day,
out cars or at the rear of a
pushing cars.
C. C. not lighted

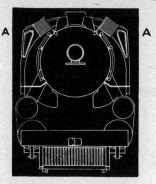

Engine running backward by
night, without cars or at the rear
of any train pushing cars.
C. C. lighted

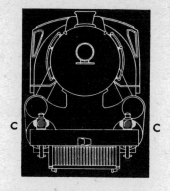

Engine running forward by day
displaying signals for a following
section.

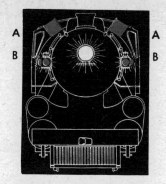

Engine running forward by night
displaying signals for a following
section.

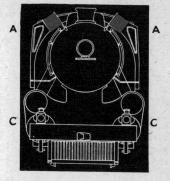

Engine running backward by day,
without cars or at the rear of a
train pushing cars, and displaying signals for a following section.
C. C. not lighted

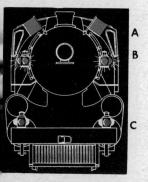

ine running backward by
t, without cars or at the rear
train pushing cars, and dis-
ing signals for a following
ion.
B. B. and C. C. lighted

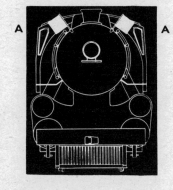

Engine running forward by day
as an extra train.

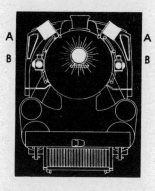

Engine running forward by night
as an extra train.
White lights at B. B.

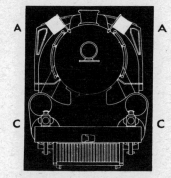

Engine running backward by day
as an extra train without cars or
at the rear of a train pushing cars.

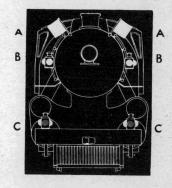

Engine running backward by
night as an extra train without
cars or at the rear of a train pushing cars.
B. B. and C. C. lighted

HAND, FLAG AND LAMP SIGNALS
The hand, or a flag, moved the same as the lamp, as illustrated gives the same indication

STOP
ng across the track.

REDUCE SPEED
Held horizontally at
arm's length, when
train is moving.

PROCEED
Raised and lowered
vertically.

BACK
Swung vertically in a circle
at half arm's length across
the track, when the train is
standing.

TRAIN HAS PARTED
Swung vertically in a circle
at arm's length across the
track, when the train is running.

APPLY AIR BRAKES
Swung horizontally above
the head when the train is
standing.

RELEASE AIR BRAKES
Held at arm's length above
the head when the train is
standing.

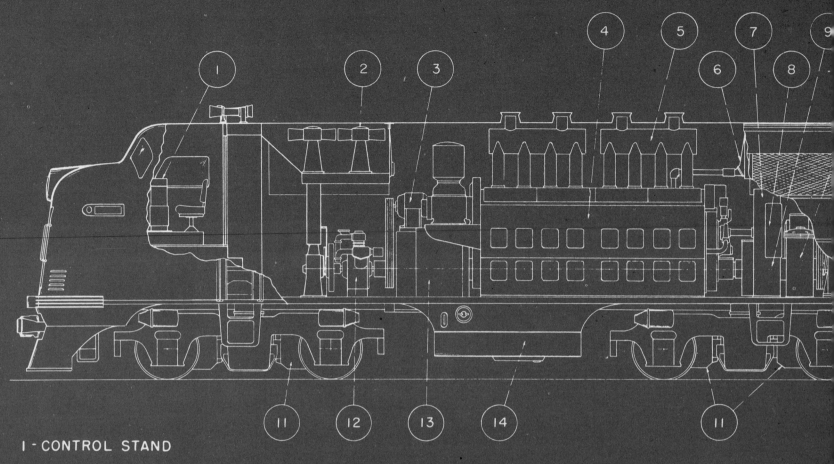

1 - CONTROL STAND
2 - COOLING FANS
3 - AUXILIARY GENERATOR
4 - 16 CYL. DIESEL ENGINE
5 - EXHAUST MUFFLER
6 - RADIATOR
7 - COOLING WATER TANK

2700 HP DIESEL-

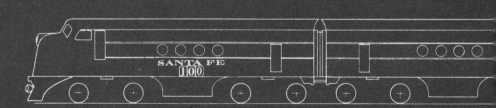

54

SAN